Zoom In on
Our Renewable Earth

Wind Power

Andrea Rivera

abdopublishing.com

Published by Abdo Zoom™, PO Box 398166, Minneapolis, Minnesota 55439. Copyright © 2017 by Abdo Consulting Group, Inc. International copyrights reserved in all countries. No part of this book may be reproduced in any form without written permission from the publisher. Abdo Zoom™ is a trademark and logo of Abdo Consulting Group, Inc.

Printed in the United States of America, North Mankato, Minnesota
102016
012017

THIS BOOK CONTAINS
RECYCLED MATERIALS

Cover Photo: Shutterstock Images
Interior Photos: Shutterstock Images, 1, 9, 10–11, 13, 18, 18–19;
Cheryl Casey/Shutterstock Images, 4; Martin D. Vonka/Shutterstock Images, 5;
Patrick Pleul/picture-alliance/dpa/AP Images, 6–7; Vaclav Vorab/Shutterstock Images, 8;
Christophe Morin/Bloomberg/Getty Images, 15; USA Art Studio/Shutterstock Images, 16–17;
Philippe Wojazer/Reuters/Newscom, 21

Editor: Emily Temple
Series Designer: Madeline Berger
Art Direction: Dorothy Toth

Publisher's Cataloging-in-Publication Data
Names: Rivera, Andrea, author.
Title: Wind power / by Andrea Rivera.
Description: Minneapolis, MN : Abdo Zoom, 2017. | Series: Our renewable Earth |
    Includes bibliographical references and index.
Identifiers: LCCN 2016948929 | ISBN 9781680799439 (lib. bdg.) |
    ISBN 9781624025297 (ebook) | ISBN 9781624025853 (Read-to-me ebook)
Subjects: LCSH: Wind power--Juvenile literature. | Wind turbines--Juvenile
    literature. | Renewable energy sources--Juvenile literature.
Classification: DDC 333.9/2--dc23
LC record available at http://lccn.loc.gov/2016948929

Table of Contents

Science

Wind is moving air.

4

It is a strong force.
Its energy can be captured.

The energy can
be changed into
electricity.

This is wind power.

Technology

Turbines capture wind power. Wind turns the blades.

They are connected to a **generator**. It turns the motion into electricity.

Engineering

Scientists use wind tunnels. The tunnels are big tubes. Fans move air through them.

Wind turbine parts are put in the tunnel. Scientists see how strong winds affect the parts.

Art

Some turbines in France look like trees. The leaves are plastic. Wind moves tiny blades inside them. Each tree can power up to 15 streetlights.

15

Math

Turbine blades can spin quickly. They might spin about 15 times every minute.

Turbine blades are long.

Many blades are more than 100 feet (30.5 m) long. They could be longer in the future.

- The first wind turbine was built in 1887.

- A group of wind turbines is called a wind farm.

- In 2015 two wind turbines were built on the second floor of the Eiffel Tower in France. They can produce enough electricity to power the first floor of the tower.

Glossary

electricity - a form of energy that can be carried through wires and power things.

energy - power that machines can use to do work.

force - a push or pull that causes a change in motion.

generator - a machine used to make electricity.

turbine - an engine that includes blades. Air, steam, or water moves the blades.

Booklinks

For more information
on wind power, please visit
booklinks.abdopublishing.com

 In on STEAM!

Learn even more with the Abdo Zoom
STEAM database. Check out
abdozoom.com for more information.

Index